SCHIRMER'S LIBRARY
OF MUSICAL CLASSICS

Vol. 1743

Henry Purcell

Keyboard Suites

Edited by
LOUIS OESTERLE

With an Introduction by
RICHARD ALDRICH

ISBN 978-0-7935-5779-0

G. SCHIRMER, Inc.

DISTRIBUTED BY

 HAL•LEONARD™
CORPORATION

7777 W. BLUEMOUND RD. P.O. BOX 13819 MILWAUKEE, WI 53213

CONTENTS

INTRODUCTORY NOTE

HENRY PURCELL was born in 1658, the son of a Gentleman of the Chapel Royal, who was also a chorister in Westminster Abbey; and himself became a chorister there in his sixth year. He, too, began his career as a composer while still a singing-boy, and came under the instruction of Blow, whom he displaced as organist of the Abbey a few years later.

His compositions, which he poured forth ceaselessly during his short life of thirty-seven years, are principally ecclesiastical and dramatic; but his instrumental music has a special significance, aside from its own inherent value, as indicating the growing predominance of Italian and French taste in England. Purcell deliberately submitted himself to its influence. He ventured upon many new and bold harmonic combinations, and left instrumental, as well as all other kinds of music, in a more highly organized and advanced stage because of his labors. His career marked the climax of the British school of music, and after his death it progressed no further.

RICHARD ALDRICH

Keyboard Suites

Suite I

Prelude.
Moderato.

Henry Purcell (1658 - 1695)
Edited by Louis Oesterle
after the edition of E. Pauer

Almand.
Andante.

42413x

Courante.
Moderato.

a)
or: In similar cases may be omitted or abbreviated.

Minuet.

* may be omitted.

4

Suite II

Prelude.
Allegro.

★ = omit.

Almand.
Moderato.

Courante.

Andante.

a)
or:

Saraband.
Sostenuto.

a) or $\text{\mancha}$ b) or $\text{\mancha}$

42413

Chacone.
Animato. (♩ = 108)

Siciliano.

42413

Suite III

Prelude.
Allegro.

Almand.
Andante.

a) or ⠶

Courante.
Moderato.

a) or 𝒘
42413

Suite IV

Prelude.
Moderato.

Almand.
Moderato.

Courante.
Moderato.

Saraband.
Sostenuto.

Suite V

Prelude.
Animato.

Almand.
Moderato.

24 Courante.
Moderato.

Saraband.
Sostenuto.

Cebell.(Gavot.)

a) or
b) or

a) or ⌣

42412

Minuet.

Riggadoon.

★) omit.

a) or 𝆺 or omit.

Intrada.

March.
Moderato.

a) or ∿

★) omit.

Suite VI

Prelude.
Moderato.

Almand.
Andante.

Hornpipe.
Moderato.

Almand.
Molto moderato.

Suite VII

Courante.

Moderato.

Hornpipe.

Suite VIII

Prelude.
Animato.

Almand.
Molto moderato.

* = omit.   a) trill from above in similar places:

Hornpipe.
Animato.

Minuet.

Almand

a) or